Divorcing Facebook?

Really!?

Audrey Wagner

Edited by Nathan A. Jacobs and Keith Buhler

Copyright © 2015 Audrey Wagner

Only with written permission from the author may parts of this book be reproduced in any form or by any electronic or mechanical means including information storage and retrieval systems. It is permissible for reviewers of this book to quote short excerpts in a review.

ISBN: 069243240X

ISBN-13: 978-0692432402
(Rural Roads Publishing)

This book reflects my experiences and thoughts as a Facebook user until I deleted my account in January of 2015 and also includes my thoughts about Facebook after that time.

Audrey Wagner

DEDICATION

This book is dedicated to those of you who will be happier without Facebook. If you are a highly sensitive person (HSP) like me, this book is dedicated particularly to you, as Facebook may often be overwhelming and anxiety-provoking for you. Divorcing Facebook may bring you a great sense of relief, happiness, and simplicity.

CONTENTS

	Acknowledgements	i
1	Is It True Love?	1
2	Soul Erosion	11
3	Too Much Real Estate	16
4	The Rent Is Too Damn High	24
5	Maybe We're Not Missing Out	32
6	One Foot in Cyberspace	43
7	The Feelings Were A Delusion	51
8	Socially Anxious	78
9	We May Want To Divorce Facebook If…	100
10	"It's Complicated"	116
11	Filing The Papers	124
12	Old Flames	130

ACKNOWLEDGMENTS

I would like to thank those who shared with me their thoughts about Facebook. I also thank Heather Jacobs for reading my first draft and offering honest, insightful comments that shaped the content and direction of my book. I am indebted to Nathan Jacobs for his thorough editing work and key suggestions. I am grateful for Keith Buhler's edits and suggestions for structure and additional content. I thank my mom for her unconditional encouragement, support, and recommendations that brought clarification and creativity to this writing project.

1
IS IT TRUE LOVE?

My first reaction to Facebook, over ten years ago, was, "Oh, neat." I began using it, assuming my use was beneficial. However, I never stopped to truly evaluate my relationship with Facebook.

I became a typical Facebook user in my ten-year relationship with the site. I checked it throughout the day, shared posts anywhere from daily to monthly, and often *like*d and commented on statuses. I used it for much of my personal messaging. I *like*d pages and shared articles, photos, and quotes. I even joined some groups. Facebook was helpful in developing my love for photography as I began posting pictures of sunsets and cornstalks. After a year of positive feedback, I bought a professional camera and started a photography page on Facebook with hopes of gaining clients for portrait photography.

I enjoyed posting my latest sunset photo, a party invite, or a status about my Saturday-morning front porch sitting. I felt connected to cousins, aunts, uncles, siblings, close friends, and acquaintances. Even my interactions with strangers meant something. And I'd be lying if I said I was not elated by the dozens of birthday greetings on my Facebook wall. I felt like a star shining a bit more brightly on my special day. *Like*s, comments, messages, and wall posts made me feel cared for and connected. These interactions were encouraging, warmed my heart, gave me desired input, and offered me some good laughs.

Yet for reasons I will begin explaining in the next chapter, I ended my relationship with Facebook. I even decided to write a book about it.

I have a twinge of guilt and a vision of an angry mob propelling tomatoes at me as I write. After all, I hear about Facebook in a positive light almost daily. People find life-changing articles, cute photos, and important news on Facebook. Facebook has made possible the saving of lives; the reunion of estranged family and friends; the finding of jobs, spouses, and abducted children; the thriving of businesses; and help and support for those in need. As the slimy insides of ruptured tomatoes slide down my clothing, know that I am happy for those who love Facebook. I hope the blessings and benefits of Facebook continue for them.

Facebook use has also led to divorce, bullying, and job loss. But even that is beside the point. Whether or not Facebook is inherently good, bad, or neutral isn't the subject of this book. The subject of this book is a particular relationship with Facebook that may be grounds for a divorce from the site. Facebook, by design, beckons us to spend more and more time on the site. It also attracts our emotional interest in being visible, influential, liked, connected, relevant, and helpful. I reflect on these and several other aspects of Facebook in the following chapters, but always for the purpose of illuminating the soul-eroding relationships that some of us have with the site. I want to provide a self-help guide of sorts for those whose relationships with Facebook are toxic—the kind of help that would have allowed me to evaluate and end my relationship with Facebook sooner.

Simply put, some people would be happier, more peaceful, and more productive without a Facebook account. I turned out to be one of those people, and I'm guessing I am not an anomaly. We have only to converse with active

Facebook users to learn that no matter how much they appear to love the site, what many of them feel for Facebook isn't exactly true love. They may post to the newsfeed often and even run pages and groups. Yet, they daydream of quitting the site. Some Facebook users, among them the most well-balanced people I know, have admitted to me the following:

- Feeling life would be more peaceful without Facebook;
- Wishing for the willpower to quit Facebook;
- Discovering things they would rather not know about their Facebook friends;
- Spending too much time on the Facebook newsfeed;

- Judging other people's posts on Facebook;
- Becoming depressed or stressed because of Facebook;
- Feeling bewildered, hurt, or angry at being unfriended on Facebook;
- Posting too often to Facebook;
- Fearing what others will think if they quit Facebook;
- Having a love/hate relationship with Facebook;
- Feeling obligated to remain on Facebook.

Just like my initial "Oh, neat," reaction, Facebook is something many people just do, without suspecting their Facebook use might be keeping them from the life they want to live.

Programs that let people block social media sites can effectively provide intermittent breaks from Facebook for specific amounts of time. I am sure they are a greatly helpful option for many folks.

Yet, my book is most likely to connect with those who would be happiest if they removed Facebook from their lives completely, who would rather not make ongoing efforts to restrict their Facebook use and who would rather not deal with the added temptation to remove social media restrictions after trying them out.

You may be one of these people. Chances are good that you've picked up my book because at least a part of you wants to quit Facebook, and you'd like to explore that possibility. Maybe the "love" you have for Facebook is actually just addiction or fear of letting go. Or maybe it's true love. My aim is to help you find out. I hope this book will help you unearth how you really feel about the site. My desire is to inspire, empower, and guide you towards a divorce from Facebook if that is what you truly want. And if you come to the end with your love of Facebook intact, at least you will have more clarity that your relationship with Facebook is something you truly desire to hold onto.

Really.

Think about your Facebook connections, and pay attention to your intuition. Do you feel happy, or do you feel unsettled in some way? When you imagine no longer being on Facebook, what feels stronger: a sense of sadness, or a sense of relief?

2
SOUL EROSION

Like many others, I joined Facebook because it was popular and stayed because I enjoyed it. But at the very end, just before I quit, I noticed I had gradually become unsettled and annoyed with the aspects of Facebook use that I describe in this book.

After deleting my account, I was dismayed when websites asked me to sign in with Facebook. Restaurant menus, rental trucks, and business signs ruffled my feathers when they asked me to find, follow, or *like* them on Facebook. When I would glimpse others' newsfeeds, memories of scrolling my own newsfeed plagued me. I had allowed my relationship with Facebook to go from "Oh, neat," to love/hate, to hate before I permanently deleted my account. I had allowed the relationship to continue long past the point when I suspected I wanted to end it. Why?

My feelings about Facebook had changed slowly and subtly, and the widespread popularity of Facebook made it easy to neglect that nagging sense that I might not, after all, want to be a Facebook user.

This nagging sense was similar to other times in my life when I had felt my soul eroding. I'd gradually feel less alive, and if this went on long enough, I'd become mildly depressed and irritable. I just didn't feel like my best self. The cause could be a job that was creating too much stress, a schedule too full to allow time for reflection, a less-than-healthy relationship, a living arrangement that wasn't working, or an obligation I wished I could take off my plate. Deep examination of these soul-eroding circumstances led me to the freedom to finally make a change.

My Facebook use had become one of those soul-eroding things for me in spite of my positive encounters on the site. I felt addicted to Facebook, checking it often. After all, I had people to follow. I had notifications to check. I had conversations and events going. I had news to keep up with. I had a never-ending stream of suggested content beckoning towards me, and I would hop from one article or page to the next. I sensed my vitality diminishing with every post, share, *like*, comment, newsfeed scroll, and page visit. My Facebook use dotted my day too frequently and kept me bobbing on the surface of life. The happiness, meaning, and excitement I experienced on Facebook were ultimately not deep enough to justify its regular and time-consuming role in my life.

My relationship with Facebook had been eroding my soul.

Is Facebook worth its potential soul-eroding effects? In the next two chapters, we will explore the inner world of Facebook and assess its cost.

Really.

When you've had soul-eroding circumstances or relationships, you may have noticed how subtle soul-erosion can be. Is your draw to the Facebook newsfeed a lifeless gravitation? Have you felt bored or listless while scrolling the newsfeed, yet kept returning to it?

3
TOO MUCH REAL ESTATE

What is Facebook?

This may sound like a philosophical question, but, fear not, I won't get into metaphysics. My Facebook use reduced the quality of my life, and I wondered why I had stayed with it so long; so, naturally, I spent a lot of time reflecting on this "thing" we call Facebook. As I pondered the nature of

Facebook, I decided the site is like a vacation rental.

I'll explain.

Facebook is not a finite location, so it can't replace our physical addresses. Rather, Facebook is "omnipresent" (or ever-present) via computers, tablets, and smartphones. With a pixelated screen in front of us, we can take up residence in this omnipresent vacation rental wherever else we might be, without even having to pack a bag.

The vacation home on our screens contains endless rooms for all of the people, groups, and interests we want to invite in. Every time we decide to make our connections official with *like*s, the cost of rent (our time) goes up. Our vacation rental is open to everyone and everything and increasingly becoming a cyber replica of the world; no matter how far apart we are on the globe, we can all "share" this home-away-from-home. A celebrity that lives on another continent is as close to us as the ice cream parlor down the street.

Of course, this vacation rental has no spatial limitations, so there is no end to the images and information scrolling within its walls. We are inundated with more than we could ever see and read if we were limited by space. Though we may choose who and what we friend and *like*, we cannot control the unwanted news, thoughts, quotes, images, and suggested content that our houseguests have in tow.

This vacation rental may be unique in its omnipresence and limitless space, but it sure isn't unique in its need for maintenance. We don't need to vacuum or fix a leaking faucet, but to get in on the action we do have to wade through numerous posts, conversations, and messages as well as choose our replies, comments, and *like*s. Our cover and profile photos need updating; Facebook groups require coordination of events and participation in a host of conversations; and our Facebook pages beckon us to post news and images in order to regularly engage our "audience" to keep them interested in our ministries or businesses. Then there are comments to reply to and to *like*. We may have messages from people who, because of our

Facebook connection, have found a reason to converse with us. We may be afraid of fading into Facebook oblivion if we neglect any of these chores. The more active we are on Facebook, the more noticeable is our absence; we may fear that our friends, page-*like*rs, or group members will feel ignored if we disappear for a while. In the end, maintaining our Facebook interactions can feel like a full-time job. We've invited all these folks in to visit; are we now going to fail to keep the party going?

This raises the question: Do we really have time for a vacation rental that beckons us to spend more and more time in it regardless of our other "real life" obligations? It's so enticing. It's crowded and stimulating; there are so many rooms to visit and a multitude of new room suggestions along the way. Yet, the more connections we make, the more we must maintain. It is hard to know when to bypass rooms, close doors, and ignore the myriad people passing us by on our left and right. We are trading our time for Facebook space. But do we really want to rent this place? Can we afford an omnipresent replica of the people and things in our lives (plus many, many more) that beckon for our time and attention?

Many of us already have too much on our plates. Our attention is spread wide and thin, our fuses are short, and our minds are all over the place. Our priorities may need evaluating. Seeing Facebook for the vacation rental that it is helps us step back from it and consider its cost. If you're like me and thought, "Oh, neat," when you began using Facebook, you may not have guessed that this fun get-away would require our most treasured asset: our time. We've been carrying this vacation rental with us everywhere we go, paying for its limitless space with the high price of our limited time.

"Oh, neat," eventually became, for me, "No, thanks."

This vacation home is one big chunk of real estate.

Really.

Visualize the people and things on your plate, and discern if your plate is crowded or spilling over. If a gigantic online social network were cleared from your plate, would there be room for one or more things you've really wanted to focus on or accomplish? Would you be able to tackle your to-do lists more efficiently?

4
THE RENT IS TOO DAMN HIGH

Because Facebook is an omnipresent, cyber rental home, which we pay for with our valuable time, it tends to—you guessed it—waste time. We touched on just how large this vacation home is, just how endless are its rooms, and how hard this real estate works to raise our rent (time) by suggesting more connections. To attain the goal of connecting us with more people and things, Facebook invites us to see information we were not seeking out originally.

Page content *like*d by friends was ever scrolling on my newsfeed, presenting more things to *like* and more content to subscribe to—photos of great photography pages, recipes on nutrition pages, content of friends' pages, and articles and quotes from self-help pages. And what about the pages of friends of friends or family members of friends? The treadmill of information never stopped moving.

As a former Facebook user, I now turn to Google for things that interest me, such as "common mineral deficiencies" and "Jaime King interviews." Starting with my genuine curiosities and then perusing information makes life so much simpler.

Likewise, I prefer going shopping only if there is something I know I want. If we took numerous trips to Walmart every day without having anything in particular to buy, we would be rightly called crazy. If I browse the entire store just in case something grabs my attention, letting every advertisement pop out and beckon to me, I not only waste a lot of time but also end up buying things I don't need. But this is exactly what we do on Facebook when we spend time perusing all kinds of people and things we never intended to check out.

But if there is something I *already know* I want, I can go into the store, grab it, go back home, and continue on with my life. Likewise, if I want to connect with a friend or read the news, I can call, write, email, or do an online search directly. Is going through Facebook the kind of time-wasting we want to sign up for permanently?

It should be a no-brainer that Facebook is making us busier. Yet, it's easy to tell ourselves that Facebook makes life simpler by having the people and things in our lives in one "location." We might use this logic to convince ourselves that we should remain Facebook users. But this is often a delusion that keeps us saddled to the site. Truth is, we connect with more people, groups, interests, and media because we are on Facebook. There is a plethora of conversations, posts, images, and updates we would not engage were it not for Facebook. Rather than just putting our social interactions all in one place, Facebook *creates* interactions. We don't have to be logicians to see the truth of this claim:

1. Facebook usage requires more interactions with more people and things.
2. Anything that requires more interactions with more people and things requires more of our time.
3. Therefore, Facebook usage requires more of our time.

How many times have we logged onto Facebook for one specific reason, gotten caught up in a post or page, and two hours later could not remember the original thing we intended to check? Those of us who have perused the Facebook newsfeed have likely concluded that the site takes up time rather than frees up time. Quitting Facebook makes this evident. Suddenly there are regular stretches of free time that were previously occupied with Facebook. Facebook not only consumes time, but it can do so in the worst possible way, through regular interruptions—new comments on our posts, new *like*s, a new event. And who has the discipline to wait until 9 p.m. to check Facebook notifications?

How do time-wasting and interruptions impact our goals? Stephen King, in his book *On Writing*, says that if you are starting out as a writer, you won't watch television; there simply isn't time for it: "[Y]ou could do worse than strip your television's electric plug-wire, wrap a spike around it, and then stick it back into the wall. See what blows, and how far. Just an idea."[1]

How serious are we about writing those books, completing those projects, or starting that business? How badly do we want to master that instrument, play with children without distractions, or visit that lonely relative? Can we afford to allow our Facebook use to take up and interrupt our precious, limited time? When we know that Facebook demands rent (time) that we can't necessarily afford, we might be more motivated to pull the plug.

It's time to think about what we already know: the rent is too damn high.

---

[1] Stephen King, *On Writing* (New York: Pocket Books, 2000), 34-35.

Really.

Many of us state that we are busy and wish we had more time. That wish can become a reality with a simple delete button. If you were to fully dive into your goals, interests, and relationships without the distractions and interruptions of Facebook, what might be the outcome?

5
MAYBE WE'RE NOT MISSING OUT

Many of us would breathe a huge sigh of relief if we had more time. So, why are we spending time in this omnipresent cyber vacation home?

We spend time on Facebook for a reason.

It's simple, really. Facebook gives us the benefit of *access*. Access to each other's profiles and posts. Access to our interests all in one place. Access to a personal "stage" for each of us, a platform all our own, so we can share who we are and what we're doing. Our access to this plethora of images, updates, and conversations depends on our ongoing relationship with Facebook. We know that if we delete our accounts, then—*poof!*—our access is gone. It's the great fear of "missing out" that keeps us from pressing *delete.*

It's true; Facebook is right. If we delete our accounts, we will indeed "miss out," just as we fear. For the rest of our lives, we will miss an absolutely enormous array of photos, statuses, witty thoughts, and articles. In fact, the list of things we will miss could stretch for miles.

The fear of missing out kept me on Facebook far too long. After much reflection, I grew to see this fear for the misleading bondage it was. I realized that we are *already* incredibly limited in the quantity of information that we can know about others.

First, a big picture perspective might help us understand just how limited we are. In 2013, the average American knew around 600 people.[2] A dump truck of sand has one billion grains of sand.[3] If each person is a grain, the world population is a little over seven dump trucks of sand—more people than I can wrap my mind around.

The approximate 600 people we each know is about 0.0000082 percent of people on the

---

[2] Andrew Gelman, "The Average American Knows How Many People?" *New York Times,* February 18, 2013, accessed November 17, 2015, http://www.nytimes.com/2013/02/19/science/the-average-american-knows-how-many-people.html?_r=0

[3] Sciforums, "The Best Visual Description of the Size of One Billion," last modified March 27, 2008, accessed November 27, 2015, http://www.sciforums.com/threads/the-best-visual-description-of-the-size-of-one-billion.79112/

planet—at most, just a tiny pinch of sand. These numbers show that each of us is "missing out" on knowing almost the entire human race that is alive at any given point. We will never even meet them, let alone see their photos, read their thoughts, and learn their favorite latte flavors.

Furthermore, we miss out in varying degrees on the moments of those we *do* know. Obviously, it isn't physically possible to have all of the people we know and love in our living rooms day and night, providing us news, humorous quips, deep thoughts, and photos of what they're doing. When we think of the amount of time we *don't* spend with the people we know (even those closest to us), we will realize how much we miss every day.

It would seem that Facebook allows us to transcend these limitations. After all, many Facebook users are primarily interacting on the site with people they already know and see regularly. Their friend lists don't consist of lots and lots of people they have never met or met only once; rather, their friend lists consist of family members, co-workers, fellow members of churches or other organizations, close friends, and casual friends. The newsfeed may seem transcendent, like a virtual living room where all of us can be together, sharing what we want, when we want.

But are we transcending our limitations as much as we think we are when we spend time on Facebook? The irony is that even within the seemingly never-ending newsfeed, we are still fraught with limitations; we are seeing only what folks carefully choose to share, and we are missing out on everything they don't share.

But maybe we're not missing out. Our limitations could help us understand more about ourselves and our purpose as human beings. Pull from your worldview what you believe makes life worth living, what you think our purpose as human beings is. Whatever you come up with, it likely is not something you'll "miss" by deleting your Facebook account with its glorious access to information about others.

Because we are finite, "missing out" is completely unavoidable. All of us are in the same boat in that we have limited time and resources. Every choice that we make necessarily excludes other choices that compete with it. Facebook may seem to open up unlimited "opportunities," things we don't want to "miss." But while scrolling the Facebook newsfeed, we are not only *still* missing endless information about others, but we are *also* missing out on whatever we'd be doing if we didn't have Facebook accounts. So, Facebook users are missing out as much as non-Facebook users. In fact, if what we've traded to make time for Facebook is something more closely tied to our purpose as human beings, then we're missing out even more.

I gave up the Facebook benefit of access; what benefit did I gain in its place?

A huge one: now not a single moment of my life is taken from me by Facebook. We all have moments and even long stretches of time in which we wonder what to do. We have often turned to Facebook at those times. After quitting Facebook, I became more aware of the moments of emptiness that would have led me to check Facebook if I still had an account. Now, free from Facebook, those moments are occupied by the following.

- Praying
- Reading
- Journaling
- Crocheting
- Listening to podcasts
- Spending time with people
- Writing
- Taking and editing pictures
- Updating my websites

- Cleaning and organizing my house
- Conquering my to-do lists
- Planning gatherings
- Researching subjects of interest online
- Attending church
- Doing yardwork
- Hiking
- Attending Meetup groups through Meetup.com

The above list touches on the most important goals and activities in my life, and I have more time for them now—uninterrupted time, at that. I can drink deeply and attentively of all the above things without notifications or a beckoning newsfeed.

Those of us who truly wish to quit Facebook would prefer to embrace the simplicity and contentment inherent within our limitations. When we have used Facebook to spend more time "with" our Facebook friends, our lives became more distracted, cluttered, busy, and perhaps even discontent at the information we still didn't have (while feeling addicted to the information we did have).

The endless access that we love on Facebook is also our downfall. It's not that Facebook has pros and cons—it's that its pros *are* its cons.

We need not be in bondage to the lie that, without Facebook, we are missing out. Instead, we can free ourselves to carefully choose what it is we don't want to miss.

Really.

Consider that no person alive has one more minute in a day than you do. What you are doing or who you are with, at every moment, is a gift unique to you; no one else in the world has your exact moment-by-moment life experiences. Do you wish to drink deeply from them, free from curiosity over what might be happening on Facebook?

6
ONE FOOT IN CYBERSPACE

Facebook can't make us miss out any less than we already do, being the finite, limited beings that we are. But, arguably, we can miss out more as a result of our Facebook use. We can miss out, in fact, on the only place we can really be: the present moment.

Those of us who have been active Facebook users know what it's like to have one foot on the ground and the other foot on Facebook—

our omnipresent vacation rental. We have entered this get-away on our iPhone screens while drinking coffee with friends. We have entered this home-away-from-home while walking down the street, trying not to run into telephone poles. We have entered this action-packed villa while eating dinner with our families; while working on papers; while at events, snapping photos to share on the newsfeed.

We have one foot on the ground and one foot in cyberspace.

It's hard to be planted in the moment when we are beckoned by endless posts and photos. The excitement is just too great. What photo might someone have posted? What update? What witty remark? What thoughtful musings?

What relationship status? What article? We were just starting to relax, but then we had to check our newsfeed. We were just settling down with a book, and then we had to see if there were any more comments or *like*s on our posts. We are half doing what we are doing and half on Facebook.

We are preoccupied with sharing our moments, which requires—*gulp*—leaping out of them. It is almost impossible to just be in a beautiful moment when we are imagining how we will share that moment in a status update, crafting a clever remark and uploading an eye-catching photo to go with it. Can we live wholeheartedly in the moment if we are juggling that moment with a post and the anticipation of *like*s and positive comments that will follow?

Something of the present moment is lost when we are busy preserving it, and using Facebook temps us to preserve far more moments than we otherwise would. If I have just seconds to capture and share a moment with my tablet's camera, how am I going to relish it myself? Our habit of preserving our moments for Facebook has become so ingrained that we work hard at it even when there are others capturing the same thing. Is my event photo really needed alongside dozens of others taken from the same angle? After all 34 of these identical photos roll on down the newsfeed, is anyone even going to look at them again? The actual event could have been enough. The real thing could have been savored. But we gave up the real thing in attempt to memorialize it and gained in its stead mere photos of something we didn't allow ourselves to fully appreciate.

If you are addicted to posting on Facebook and proceed to delete your account, you might be amazed at how deeply you can dive into your moments. Imagine that there will be nothing to capture, preserve, duplicate, or share with regards to Facebook. No *like*s or comments. No notifications. No status updates. Just you and your moments.

The present moment has profound value when we can drink it in without distraction, with both feet planted on the ground. We have the ability to be satisfied with what is. But our

Facebook use empowers us to dart out of our moments so that we can–quick!–share them in cyberspace.

How will the moment we share be valuable to someone else if we are not fully living in it ourselves? Is a moment we aren't willing to dwell in ourselves really going to alter the life of someone who sees our post about it? Our witty or thoughtful posts about our moments, which we leapt away from to capture, most often are not as life-changing or significant as we think they are. Consider that the person reading our updates also has just one foot on the ground and the other in cyberspace. Chances are good that people are not fully present when engaging our posts because they, too, are reading them with a view as to whether to *like* or comment on them. And, generally speaking, the time and interest they invest in our posts is likely not any more than the time and interest we invest in theirs.

We could be making our lives shallower because of Facebook. Some of us are so excited about the endless opportunities for sharing moments that we miss out on the finest opportunity—the present moment.

Really.

If you are like me, then photo sharing is something you want to hold onto; you may have adorable photos of your kids and pets or inspiring photos of nature scenes you snapped while taking a walk. If you didn't have a Facebook account, would you mail out prints more often, send out email newsletters with your favorite images, add more photography to your website, or have more photos made into wall art to inspire your guests? You might fall even more in love with these personal, hands-on, or creative photo-sharing opportunities that thrive apart from Facebook.

7

THE FEELINGS WERE A DELUSION

Some of us have announced our plan to delete our Facebook accounts. We are tired of the maintenance, time-wasting, and endless access of the site, not to mention the compulsion to capture and share. But months and years go by, and we still find ourselves on Facebook.

Googling "Facebook makes me sad" is one way to find articles about negative emotions related to Facebook use. We can feel jealous, depressed, and unhappy because of Facebook. But our positive feelings on Facebook might have more impact on us than our negative ones—after all, our positive feelings on Facebook are what have us addicted to the site. These good feelings have accompanying beliefs and fears that keep us from deleting our accounts.

I had feelings of happiness when using Facebook. Facebook helped me feel visible, influential, liked, connected, relevant, and helpful. Though there may have been some truth to these things, my feelings were largely a delusion. The feelings were like air balloons that loomed in the sky above while tiny kernels of truth sat humbly on the ground below.

Those of us who want to quit Facebook will benefit from a close examination of our positive feelings on Facebook. We may be motivated to finally pull the plug if we see that most of what we feel on Facebook exists more in our feelings than it does in reality.

Delusion #1: Visible

We are "seen" on Facebook by a whole lot of people at once, and we can each feel like the center of the universe. Frequent and attention-seeking posts and photos especially give this impression. Our Facebook profiles are the stars; comments, *like*s, and posts are the planets orbiting around us, making us feel significant. To feel like the center of the universe is a temptation in our *non*-Facebook lives. The ability to set up camp in a cyberspace that lets us feel like the center of our own digital universe can heighten this temptation.

People are vying to be seen in a massive sea of Facebook visibility. Are we as visible as we believe we are when visibility is something that everyone else has, too? Perhaps with so many people striving to be visible in a common cyberspace, we aren't as visible as we imagined. Rather, we are each getting lost in the visibility crowd. But we can feel oh-so-visible when we are at our own profile pages, maintaining our various photos, posts, *like*s, and interests and seeing ourselves on the newsfeed. We can easily forget that we are each just another fish in a sea of visibility.

It can feel good to have a Facebook profile, a representation of ourselves for all to see—a carefully chosen photo to serve as an icon of who we are; posts and photos to the newsfeed that represent what we are willing to show of ourselves; a sense that we have a stage and an audience. Perhaps many of us aren't that vain, and we don't think we want or need this visibility. We might still ask ourselves if visibility on Facebook makes us feel good in some way. If it does, we may have an accompanying fear that deleting Facebook will make us less visible. In either case, the visibility Facebook makes possible may boost pressure to remain on the site.

Delusion #2: Influential

We want our influence to reach others. We want others to read our deep thoughts and quotes, click on the links to our blog posts, and see our shared articles. In our fog of excitement about our influence on Facebook, we may forget a few things.

First, our friends are more excited about their own influence on Facebook than they are about ours. Facebook is the stage for each one of us to show who we are. We use it to put ourselves, our thoughts, our skills, our products, or our ministries "out there." If being influential is our aim, then in all likelihood we are logging onto Facebook to influence others more than to be influenced ourselves. If our cyber friends are anything like us in this regard, then our influence is likely less than we hope.

Second, our "influence" on Facebook is competing with a host of other influences in a distracting environment. Our voice is part of a cacophony of voices that are seeking to influence. Therefore, each of us appears to be clamoring. In an environment so noisy, is our audience in a good place to deeply absorb that influential quote, thought or blog post we shared? Does a *like* amount to influence? With so many opportunities for engagement on Facebook, our audience may not be terribly interested in our posts. But even if they are, they can't give their undivided attention to them while they are taking a sneak peek at the remainder of the newsfeed and getting interrupted by notifications.

Thirdly, we are desensitized to profundity when it comes to Facebook. Profound posts aren't so profound anymore when we are used to seeing them on the newsfeed. Furthermore, our spiritual posts are sandwiched between football highlights and coupons for stiletto heels. We are trivializing our influence when we spread it on Facebook, where, like a flea market, the street preacher on the corner is ignored while the cheap jewelry a few yards away is selling like hotcakes.

We may think Facebook is the perfect venue to get ourselves "out there" and make a difference in the world. After all, "everyone" is camped there, so it's the best place to reach people. Right?

It may seem so. But we are probably not changing the world by being on Facebook, given how loud and crowded an environment it is. Is it possible that living out our convictions could have a greater impact than posting about our convictions? Perhaps praying has more power than posting about the power of prayer. Perhaps who we actually are makes more of an impact than our posts about who we think we are. Perhaps doing something to combat a social injustice does more than posting about social injustice.

Perhaps our influence on Facebook is not so influential.

Delusion #3: Connected

Whether we are religious or into theories of psychology, most of us believe that close, loving relationships are integral to the purpose of our existence. Other than sociopaths, who doesn't want to be connected?

The convenience of Facebook helps us do more interacting with more people than we would have the ability to do otherwise. We can build and expand relationships on the edifice of Facebook posts, comments, and *like*s. We might not have the motivation or courage for these same interactions if they required more work. But within the buffer of a large social network, it's socially acceptable to do quite a bit of conversing and *lik*ing.

Phone calls, emails, and in-person visits are just so—*personal*. They require courage and a certain comfort level. So when Facebook allows us to bypass those and expand our social lives in cyberspace, we are so much more connected. Right?

More online interactions may not be making us more connected for several reasons.

Our "selves" on Facebook are representations of ourselves that often don't show who we really are. We select the statements, photos, and content we want others to see. If we do lots of interacting on Facebook without letting our deeper selves be seen, we may imagine we are more connected while we are actually feeling lonelier.

Our connections on Facebook are less intentional when we are not directing our representations of ourselves to any one person in particular. We sling our witty, poetic, or mundane thoughts into cyberspace and wait to see who might attend and respond. How connected are we with others when our communication isn't directed at any one of them individually?

Facebook might be more about our feelings of connectedness than about real, intimate encounters. Facebook can feel like a happening party where we are excited about our common location, and we soon find ourselves drunk on our mutual feelings of connectedness and sharing. We are excited we are at this vacation rental "party." We are excited that this party is making it possible for us all to have a good time. We are excited about the buzz of status updates and *like*s. Yet, maybe what we are connecting with most at this party is not each other but rather our feelings about interactions made possible by Facebook.

The sense of connectedness we feel on Facebook is often the outcome of trivial banter. We most likely were not seeking the conversations we find. Rather, we got involved in this or that conversation because we checked our newsfeeds. Spare moments in my day were spent learning what restaurant friends were at; that someone else safely arrived in Florida; that an acquaintance I haven't seen in ten years picked out a Christmas tree with her family; that my aunt's plumbing is bad in her new house; about GMO ingredients in baby formula; that the Pope's latest comment sounded too much like Universalism; or how cute my baby nephew is in his pumpkin suit.

Maybe our feelings of connectedness on Facebook have deluded us.

Delusion #4: Liked

Any of us who can be even slightly funny, thoughtful, or cute is bound to get *like*s for our photos and posts on Facebook. The *like* button is nothing less than brilliant in its appeal to humanity. Moreover, the button is easy-as-pie to press—the quickest way ever invented to make someone feel liked.

Who doesn't want to give someone an easy and instant pick-me-up? It makes us feel good to *like* others' posts. We may feel closer to them. We may experience a noble sense of charity. We may be hopeful of getting *like*s in return. And those of us being *like*d might experience elation. We may feel instantly better about ourselves. We may feel connected. We may feel good about how easy it is to be liked in cyberspace. If only it had been this easy in the seventh grade.

This pick-me-up button gives everyone involved a like "fix."

In our foggy haze of *I'm-liked* feelings, reality can get a little misty. The thing is, the *like* button can mean a lot of things. One of those things, of course, is, "I like your post."

Here are some other things the *like* button can mean:

- Let's pretend that catastrophic attempt at being roommates never happened.
- No one else has *like*d your post, and I feel sorry for you.
- You stood me up for coffee last week, but I'm willing to forget about that.
- I am doing my *like* rounds for the day, and your post made the cut.
- I want to marry you.
- I'm really hoping you'll ask me to housesit for you next weekend.
- I'm really hoping you'll babysit for me *this* weekend.
- It's Friday night, and I have nothing to do.

- We both know neither one of us is excited about seeing each other at that family reunion next week.

The *like* button can, of course, reflect genuine like, as we have all experienced. But it can also simply mean little to nothing. Or it can be the expression of myriad motives or even a defense mechanism against feelings of dislike. For example, a couple of friends of mine regularly *like*d the posts of someone they strongly disliked. The *like* button can serve as a convenient buffer or pretense between us and those with whom we don't actually want to be connected.

Being *like*d on Facebook can become an addiction. In moments of emptiness or loneliness, we only have to post the first thoughtful or witty statement that comes to mind, and *voila*, we have collected some *like*s and are feeling better.

We may in fact be liked. But is the *like* button how we know that? It might mislead us about how others truly feel about us and our posts. The *like* button helps us merely *feel* more liked, but it may not be an accurate barometer of how others perceive us.

Is this magical button worthy of our positive feelings?

The *like* button is doing one thing for sure: lifting us higher up into the *like*s air balloon. But while on this joy ride, we can lose sight of the ground below.

The additional Facebook "emoji" reactions to posts certainly provide more variation and nuance; in addition to *like*, Facebook users can express love, laughter, celebration, surprise, sadness, and anger, and they may have more or different options in the future. Of course, these more specific "emojis" can be used with complete sincerity. Yet, unfortunately, these additional "emojis" are not substantially different from the *like* button in the sense that they can be used pretentiously and with various motives.

Delusion #5: Relevant

Facebook recruits every person and thing on the whole planet to have a presence on the site. The key phrase here is *the whole planet*. The internet.org initiative to provide free basic internet access (including Facebook) to the entire inhabited earth is led by—you guessed it—Facebook.[4] This incredible pervasiveness implies that if we are human, we need to be on the site, too. After all, do we want to be left out of this cyberspace replica of reality? If so, we might just become irrelevant. Our visibility and social lives and ministries might dissolve into oblivion. Everyone else will be noticed, but we will be forgotten. How will people "find" us if we aren't on Facebook? How will they "see" us? Facebook is that vacation rental to which we've invited everyone to hang out. If we don't hang out there, too, we'll miss the party. We won't be

---

[4] Facebook, "Our Approach," Internet.org by Facebook, https://info.internet.org/en/ (accessed January 19, 2016).

in the loop on the large chunk of updates and social interactions that occur in people's lives.

The more active we've been on Facebook, the more our vacation home feels like planet earth—and the more we see in pixels.

Let's first remind ourselves that everyone on Facebook can be reached through email. Most people have phone numbers and addresses, too. And businesses or ministries that are represented by Facebook pages typically have websites. So, we can certainly be relevant apart from Facebook.

Second, it's easy to forget that the ground we are walking on is the real thing and that there are a myriad of other ways we can "show up" on this planet besides being on Facebook. Being relevant outside of Facebook is downright classy. It means being relevant in our own spaces rather than sharing our spaces with an extremely large, clamoring crowd. The principle of scarcity tells us that we value things more when they are not easily attainable in abundance. Therefore, when people have to exert the incredible effort it takes to visit our websites, they may value us *more*. When they can't find us on Facebook, they may even get butterflies because we are playing a little hard to get.

Remember the cost of renting space in this vacation home. We pay with our time, we live distracted, and we fear missing out. This is a high price to pay in exchange for the delusion of relevance. The societal pressure to be relevant on Facebook is a puff of worthless smoke, and we can watch it dissipate if we click *delete*. The very best way to dispel this delusion is to divorce Facebook and then see just how relevant we remain.

Delusion #6: Helpful

A friend told me the students in her singles outreach were on Facebook, "so I guess I need to be on Facebook, too." She reasoned she would get more student attendance to the meetings if she joined Facebook.

Many of us have created pages and groups on Facebook to help gain more involvement for our outreaches. We may feel the need to use Facebook because "that is where everyone is." We figure there will be more conversations, events, interactions, and attention paid to us. Perhaps our group meetings will get more attendance. Being active on Facebook for these reasons might feel honorable, like we're reaching out and meeting others where they are at, hoping to help them by becoming more like them.

We have to ask ourselves, however, how it is we are helping them.

First, we are catering to their preferred social platform. We are affirming their decision to be active on Facebook. Is that truly helping them? Are we doing something noble? We are helping them in one way for certain: we are helping them log onto Facebook more frequently. Is this admirable?

Secondly, we are adding more clutter to their already-busy newsfeeds. We are trying to get their attention by dividing their attention even further. We might seem like a breath of fresh air if we *can't* be found on Facebook. Away from the noisy Facebook marketplace, people might even take us more seriously.

But if others don't value us enough to visit our websites, call us up, send us emails, or approach us in person, that's okay, too. They are just as responsible for connecting with us as we are for connecting with them. If our absence from Facebook makes them forget about our outreaches, they may not be too interested in being reached out to—which means they probably don't want our "help."

If we decide we want to quit Facebook, the fact that almost everyone else is on the site is a moot point. We help neither them nor ourselves by staying on Facebook if the site isn't right for us.

We may, however, help others by divorcing Facebook. If we quit the site, we might inspire others who want to do the same.

***

That cyber rope tying me to Facebook, through which I felt visible, influential, liked, connected, relevant, and helpful, was woven of hollow emotional highs. My presence on Facebook didn't have the significance I felt it had.

The feelings were a delusion.

Really.

You may find that your feelings on Facebook are meaningfully connected to what you are experiencing on the site, or, if you are like me, your feelings on Facebook have been more akin to shallow pick-me-ups. Does feeling visible, influential, liked, connected, relevant, or helpful drive you to use Facebook frequently? If so, you may find that your positive feelings on Facebook could be controlling your Facebook usage more than you hoped.

8
SOCIALLY ANXIOUS

Busy and distracted in our omnipresent vacation rental, emotionally sucked in and afraid to leave, it's not unreasonable to consider that we might be getting anxious. After all, we are "managing" a large aspect of our social lives in this get-away rental, so our relational dynamics are at play around the clock. There are more people, more conversations, and more opportunities to encourage each other.

We also have more opportunities to *collide* with each other.

Facebook enables many positive encounters. Sadly, our Facebook use can also set us up for conflict, jealousy, and misunderstandings. Hot-button topics, critical comments, unfriendings, and people airing their hurts on the newsfeed are just a few examples of the negativity on Facebook that creates stress for many users.

Relationships sometimes lack harmony. It's easy to offend, judge, misunderstand, and annoy—we have all been on both sides of these conflicts. Some of us, however, tend to get a bit more anxious in social situations. We strive to say the right things and avoid upsetting others. We prefer peace; negativity doesn't roll off our backs easily. We are sensitive souls, profoundly aware when harmony is disrupted. For those of us in this camp, Facebook has the potential to be a significant source of stress. For us, even if most of our encounters on Facebook are positive, we may not feel that the following anxiety-provoking dilemmas make Facebook worth it in the long run.

The Unfriending Dilemma

Conflict with others can create anxiety. There is the rude person at work, the neurotic roommate, and the person we thought we were dating who was actually friend-zoning us.

These scenarios are sticky and painful enough without adding cyberspace dynamics. When one of these conflicts happens to us, we may hear that mental drumroll: Is this person going to unfriend us? Should *we* do the unfriending? Or should we remain Facebook friends and just take a siesta from clicking *like* on each other's posts? When our non-cyber relationships are on the rocks, what will become of the *cyber* versions of these relationships?

We type the names of these people into the Facebook search bar with hopes of not finding those two dreaded words, *Add Friend*, beneath. If they still are our friends on Facebook, then there's the burning question of if/when an unfriending might still occur and who will execute it.

I-was-unfriended-and-don't-know-why is a spin-off of this dilemma. Maybe we didn't make the cut when others did their Facebook-friend house cleaning. Or maybe we were unfriended quite intentionally. Either way, *ouch*. If the sting could speak, it might say, *This person is making our disconnect official*. It's akin to a cyber-restraining order. Although in our non-Facebook lives we don't expect everyone to like us, it's nice when that understanding is not as concrete as it is on Facebook. We might feel the need to avoid each other at the farmer's market now that there has been an unfriending. But if not for Facebook, we might have exchanged pleasant small talk while picking out ripe tomatoes.

The final spin-off of this dilemma is the Facebook friends we're not actually friends with. They might be remote acquaintances. The lurking question is, *Should we unfriend them?* If so, what if we run into them at malls or grocery stores? What if they turn up at the parties we are invited to? Will they notice they've been unfriended? And if so, will they know it wasn't anything personal? Where is the line between acquaintances and people we've met only once? Considering all these questions can hurt our brains. It hurt mine.

Having deleted my Facebook account, I am no longer connected to anyone in cyberspace. I have experienced great relief and a reduction in both confusion and anxiety. Remember, unfriending and being unfriended can be occasions for stress.

The Friend-You-to-Date-You Scenario

For those of us who are single, our Facebook use may create awkward dating scenarios. A person who has romantic interest in us may friend us on Facebook and then act like he or she is addicted to our posts, *lik*ing and commenting on every one of them. A single male friend of mine shared, "I do get a lot of people adding me just to try to date me and that is awkward, particularly if I have no interest back for them and they are *lik*ing all of my photos and statuses!"

We get asked for dates.

We say no.

Or we say yes. But the relationship doesn't work out.

No matter the scenario, we'll never forget that Facebook is where it began. And this friend-you-to-date-you scenario often leads to unfriendings from one party or the other.

I'll never forget the friend-me-to-date-me guy who friended me and ultimately asked me for three dates but never for a fourth. Awkward. Did I want to spend the rest of my Facebook days seeing his thoughts, photos, and new relationships? No. So I unfriended him. When I saw him at a restaurant a year later, we exchanged awkward pleasantries while the *I-*

unfriended-you elephant in the room stared us down.

A spinoff of this friend-you-to-date-you scenario is the people-we-have-crushes-on scenario.

Some of us remove posts and comments seconds, minutes, hours, or even days after we post them if we decide later they are silly—especially if we posted them to impress a crush.

I well remember the crush I most interacted with on Facebook—my witty remarks, selective *like*s on just the right number of his comments, and event invites. My clever party descriptions and perfectly chosen event photos were strategic in winning him over. I posted my favorite Alison Krauss song to the newsfeed, hoping he might listen and get the same wistful feelings the song gave me. And should I make my birth year visible on my profile? My age wasn't my best selling point with this guy.

When the "In A Relationship" status appeared on his profile, I knew our witty exchanges had been more significant in my head than they had been in reality. When it was all said and done, I wasn't any closer to walking down the aisle with my crush.

Another single male friend told me that flipping through Facebook photos of love interests makes it easy to go down rabbit trails of imaginary relationships. He said the format of Facebook encourages the impulse to binge-surf profiles and that it's easy to do it obsessively.

Those of us with social anxiety are bound to find these Facebook love-interest scenarios a bit uncomfortable. We try to get the attention of our crushes on Facebook. We visit their profiles. We *like* their posts. But in the end, we do it because everyone else does it, too. The truth is, many of us would prefer not to do any dating—or even crushing—on Facebook. We tire of trying to discern the social economy of how many *like*s is equal to a compliment or whether a *poke* is flirting. We weary of checking the newsfeed with curiosity about our crush's posts. We are done using *like*s and comments to try to get to know someone. A bike ride past our crush's house would feel like a breath of fresh air next to the stuffy maze of cyberspace. In this era of Facebook, we may even look back wistfully on tee-peeing and prank calls.

The Ex-Stalking Scenario

Many of us are tempted to Facebook-stalk past love interests. The ex-stalking scenario is bound to affect almost any Facebook user with a pulse. To be tempted to Facebook-stalk an ex, all we need is a normal dose of curiosity and an ex who wants to be friends with us on Facebook (or has a public profile). If we want to know what an ex is doing, or who an ex is romantically involved with, we can often access his or her information and photos with just a few clicks.

Ex-stalking on Facebook has a nebulous definition. If I am merely *tempted* to look up an ex on Facebook, does that make me an ex-stalker? What if I visit his profile only once and then never look at it again? *Then* am I an ex-stalker? Or would I have to visit his profile regularly? If I am friends with an ex on Facebook, is it wiser to follow him or to unfollow him? Is scrolling the newsfeed to see if he has a post considered ex-stalking? Having to entertain these questions sure wasn't one of the perks of being a Facebook user.

There was one ex-boyfriend in particular whose life I didn't want to be privy to. So I didn't look him up to find out whether he had joined Facebook. However, his new wife's profile appeared on my People You May Know list. My stomach was in knots over the mere possibility that I could click on her profile and see things that were none of my business to see. I couldn't remove her fast enough from my People You May Know list.

I am single, and I know that married folks are also affected by the ex-stalking scenario. For example, a married guy friend shared with me the following: "I find myself curious about my ex-girlfriends. Are they married now? Do they have kids? And do they ever Facebook-stalk me to see pictures of my kids? Even though I am happily married now, I wonder about past relationships. I'm not sure it's healthy, but Facebook makes it possible to wonder. I would be fine running into them in real life, but the online cyber-stalking vibe is very weird."

Along similar lines, a happily married female friend confessed to me that she has searched for ex-boyfriends on Facebook and looked at their photos to find out what was going on in their lives, in spite of the fact that doing so aroused in her romantic feelings and jealousy.

The mere temptation of Facebook ex-stalking can be a source of anxiety for both single and married folks. If we act on it and see news and photos of people we were once romantically connected to, unwanted feelings of nostalgia, jealousy, or even rejection could heighten our anxiety. In truth, many of us would feel better if Facebook-stalking wasn't a possibility. When this is the case, Facebook may need to get the boot.

The Rear-an-Ugly-Head

Don't we love it when the people we're not really friends with, the ones who never interact with us on Facebook, one day rear an ugly head for the sole purpose of disagreeing with our posts?

If she had previously acknowledged my existence on Facebook, then it would have been understandable for her to attack my post. But she was dead silent all the way up to the moment she disagreed with the article I posted on hidden MSG ingredients. Though I'd never received a *like* or comment from her in prior years, she decided to express that she thinks MSG is perfectly healthy.

The rear-an-ugly-head scenario happened to someone else I know. Her playful post about a political billboard was taken out of context by one of her Facebook friends. The girl who attacked her post had rarely talked to her outside of Facebook and had never talked to her on Facebook until the attack. She was offended. Truth was, the girl who posted about the billboard was trying to be humorous to impress one of her guy friends. She wasn't politically opinionated and wasn't trying to make a political statement.

The rear-an-ugly-head scenario may be quite an unpleasant surprise for those of us who are sensitive souls.

The Number-of-Likes

I got a bit too excited about *like*s on my photos and posts, so excited that I would check for new *like*s often—*too* often.

My love of photography was growing. At local farms, I photographed goats, horses, chickens, cats, and, most of all, cows. My love of capturing the cows' expressions up close made me wild for *like*s on Facebook. I'd post a cow picture late at night and be eager the next morning to see how many *like*s came after I'd gone to bed. I checked for *like*s first thing in the morning, even before I jumped in the shower.

Seriously?

When there is thrill over *like*s, then the converse can happen: getting less *like*s than usual can lead to sadness, and not getting *like*s from specific individuals can bring on the blues. It's easy to read too much into *like*s as well as into the absence of them. Were my cow greeting cards obnoxious? How come one of them got twenty-three *like*s and the other only got seven? The socially-anxious mind is left to fill in the gap where a *like* is missing.

The Facebook Page

The Facebook page can become a socially-anxious person's nightmare.

We create pages, and the supposed value for them is connected to how many people view our posts and—*gulp*—*like* our pages. We are prompted on Facebook to invite our friends, one by one, to *like* our pages. Some people who *like*d our pages at one point in the past reappear on the list of people to invite to *like* them; this tells us who our un*like*rs were. In addition, we are provided on Facebook with painful information: a specific section of our pages shows us how many un*like*s our pages have had and when they occurred.

Ouch. I learned which of my friends were less than enthralled with in-your-face cow photos.

If we say "yes" to Facebook by re-inviting our page's un*like*rs, they might think we are not willing to be un*like*d. Perhaps our un*like*rs will then fear they'll find us in their kitchens, boiling their pets on the stove. Or perhaps they didn't know that their un*like* of our page was information we had access to via Facebook, and they had no intention of communicating hurt or rejection through the un*like*.

***

Widespread use of Facebook might have us think we should be able to handle the stresses of the site—that we should be less sensitive; that we should not be so anxious; that we should let the negatives roll off our backs. This is a lot of *shoulds*. Perhaps we sensitive souls need only one *should*: we should stop *should*ing on ourselves when it comes to Facebook. Anxiety can be a clue that a situation in our lives isn't good for us. We may be better off divorcing Facebook.

Really.

Have you noticed you have many nuances in your levels of closeness with each of your friends, family members, and acquaintances? You might avoid certain topics around some of them, keep others at arm's length, and invite yet others freely into your world. Do you ever feel cramped, awkward, or stressed in a cyberworld where the only possible relationship standings are friend, follow, unfollow, and unfriend?

9
WE MAY WANT TO DIVORCE FACEBOOK IF…

At this point in the journey, you may have decided your Facebook use has wasted your time, pulled you from present moments, induced fear, and caused you stress. You may have realized all those positive feelings were a delusion and that you're just not "feeling it" anymore. If this is where you are, then I am glad I was able to help you uncover the true nature of your relationship with Facebook, and what I have to say from here will just be the cherry on top of your I-can't-wait-to-quit-Facebook ice cream Sunday.

There are yet more reasons you might want to quit Facebook. Some of us have personality traits, life circumstances, or values that make Facebook a bit too negative for us. It would be great if we weren't adversely affected by our Facebook use, but that isn't always possible. Consider the following.

WE MAY WANT TO DIVORCE FACEBOOK
IF... *we have eccentric families.*

When a family member of mine posted inappropriate pictures of his wife on the

Facebook newsfeed, he believed he was being sentimental. Entirely too much was showing in these photos. Some people aren't trying to be jerks; rather, they really just aren't very smart.

Unfortunately, these pictures included a couple of especially graphic shots. Several family members called him up and asked him to take the pictures off Facebook. He woke up from his nap to answer these calls. He replied he would take the photos down later—after his nap. He went back to sleep.

One family member left the guy a voicemail, saying he was no longer welcome at our family reunions. Another family member threatened, via text message, to fly to this guy's hometown and beat him up.

I reported the photos to Facebook and then proceeded to comment on them. My comment said, "These pictures are totally inappropriate. Take them down NOW."

A family member called to let me know that my comment, along with the graphic photos, went onto *my* newsfeed. (I had forgotten that would happen.)

Two hours later, this eccentric relative woke up from his nap and took the pictures down.

Maybe some of us have experienced even worse. Humiliating family scenarios often find their way onto Facebook. Friends of mine have been quite embarrassed by family members oversharing about their love lives, posting humiliating photos, and airing their dirty laundry and conflicts.

For those of us with "crazy family stories," some of that craziness will probably leak onto Facebook. How do we feel about that? Embarrassing posts, not to mention tags, might just make Facebook too anxiety-ridden for us. Enough embarrassment enough times could mean it is time to divorce Facebook.

WE MAY WANT TO DIVORCE FACEBOOK IF... *we have ever deactivated our accounts.*

I deactivated Facebook twice in my ten-year relationship with it. During each deactivation period, I took time to recover from the numerous negatives mentioned in this book, until I was finally ready to return to Facebook, feeling refreshed from time off the site. My need to deactivate was a warning signal that Facebook wasn't for me. However, I wasn't ready to give up feeling visible and connected to others. I hadn't yet realized that my feelings on Facebook were a delusion.

I created a new account each time I got back on the site, which necessitated re-friending everyone, one by one. A couple of people didn't accept my friend request the third time around. Can I blame them?

Numerous friends of mine have deactivated their accounts for a time, often following major life stressors. They may not have wanted to "face" Facebook in the aftermath of a terrible divorce or other relationship fallout. Who wants to be Facebook-stalked because people hope to find out more of the ugly details?

Then there are those who are always talking about quitting Facebook. They post recurring statuses about reasons to quit the site. They mention in person that they are thinking of quitting. They say they feel down after being on Facebook or are bored with the site. They feel it's a waste of time.

I understand. I've been there.

When we have deactivated our accounts in the past, that means Facebook "got" to us; we needed to escape it for a while. Consider that those feelings are likely to emerge for us again. We don't want to become like those who break up and get back together over and over again with the same person. Those of us who have talked about quitting the site already know that quitting is right for us. It may be time for a divorce from Facebook.

WE MAY WANT TO DIVORCE FACEBOOK
IF... *we don't want to exclude anyone.*

I received many event invites when I was on Facebook, but now that I'm not on the site, I'm sometimes left out. I know the host of these events intends to invite me. But he or she has forgotten that I'm not on Facebook and sometimes forgets to email or call me with an invite. Sometime I'm remembered at the last minute, but sometimes I'm not remembered until the parties are already over.

Do I question whether these hosts are really my friends? No. I know they are. But with almost everyone and everything on Facebook, it's easy to forget those few people who are not on the site.

Ironically, Facebook events are often created in hopes of including more people in a simple way, using just one platform. But the reality is, not everyone is on Facebook. Do we want to exclude the handful of people who aren't? Facebook can actually make things more complicated when we have to use both email and Facebook invites.

If we want to include everyone important to us in our announcements, invites, and conversations, then Facebook may not be for us.

Consider my friend who became active on Facebook to become relevant to her singles outreach. She is now spending a lot of time on Facebook, sharing news, prayer requests, and photos of her family on the newsfeed. Because it is easier for her to share these important things on Facebook, she isn't contacting her close friends via phone and email as often as she once did. Time spent on Facebook can become a substitute for contacting friends individually. There is less time for such contacts after time spent on Facebook, and the ones neglected are the ones not on Facebook.

Some of us fear that our social interactions on Facebook are causing our non-Facebook friends to slide off the grid. We may want to divorce Facebook so that all the people in our lives are on the same playing field.

WE MAY WANT TO DIVORCE FACEBOOK IF... *we have been annoyed by Facebook.*

Unfortunately, many things I've seen and read on Facebook have been annoying (my own posts included). Sadly, Facebook provides temptations to judge others. Sometimes we discover others' mishaps on Facebook.

A friend of mine found out through a Facebook tag that a close friend from states away came to her town for a visit and didn't tell her or see her when she was there.

Another friend said she couldn't afford to pay for the pet-sitting that friends did for her for free, but flaunted on Facebook a diamond necklace with its multi-thousand dollar price tag—a birthday gift from her husband.

Another girl told me she was too busy with schoolwork to come to our book discussion group. But Facebook revealed she was at Applebee's with her friends for dinner while the book group took place.

A friend of mine swore he'd cut things off with his psycho ex-girlfriend. But he posted a photo soon after that she had just taken of him, revealing they were still hanging out.

An acquaintance of mine started a page for her art and posted recurring threats to anyone who might be tempted to steal her work.

A few friends posted their complaints about an unknown "someone," and we readers were left to speculate who their complaints might be about.

Facebook exposes us to things we would be better off not knowing. Some of us are highly motivated to avoid scenarios that annoy us and tempt us to judge. Facebook might simply not be for us.

WE MAY WANT TO DIVORCE FACEBOOK
IF... *we are perfectionists.*

We perfectionists like everything to look and sound just right as well as be orderly. We like to do everything *really well*. The already-required maintenance of a Facebook account, not to mention groups or pages we've created, might compel us to work overtime.

I wanted my cover photo and profile picture to be positioned perfectly, color coordinated, and up to date with that particular phase of my life.

People would pop into my mind whose posts I hadn't *liked* for some time, and to keep things consistent, I'd visit their pages and make sure to *like* something. I would review my latest posts and comments to make sure they were worded well. After all, if a sentence *can* be made better, why not make it better?

For those of us who are perfectionists, tweaking and updating things until they are "perfect," we may not need one more thing in our lives to maintain. We tend to be thorough by perfecting photos and posts and crafting the wittiest remarks. We may not know when to stop checking Facebook for "maintenance" needs. We may just want to take this large chunk of cyber-maintenance off our plates. We may want to consider divorcing Facebook.

Really.

Has Facebook-related hurt, embarrassment, or annoyance ever been among your stressors? If you didn't have a Facebook account, would your stressors be fewer? Would you be relieved if Facebook could never again add to them?

10
"IT'S COMPLICATED"

I hope this little book has helped you unearth how you really feel about Facebook. You are either closer to cutting the Facebook cord, or you have decided that you want to keep renting space in this vacation home. I hope what you've read here has brought some clarity to the direction you want to take.

For some of you who want to quit Facebook, you may be ready to put down this book, get out of your chair, and permanently delete your account right now. If that's you, skip to the next chapter.

For others, you're not quite there. You may feel fairly certain you want to divorce the site, but inwardly you are wincing. After all, as the song goes, breaking up is hard to do. You think to yourself the relationship has been convenient. You worry that there will be a cost to ending it. The good moments and fond memories make you reluctant to part with it. And yet, this relationship has slowly eroded your soul and stripped you of your happiness, freedom, and vitality. You dream of being free. You agonize that there seems to be no way to pull back on the relationship just a little. Just as in any divorce, it must be a total break. That means you must walk away from the convenience and benefits to finally be free of the bad, soul-killing parts. In a real-life toxic relationship, we know that the other person's good looks or great sense of humor aren't enough to justify staying. Yet it can be hard to see that the benefits of Facebook don't justify staying with it if our relationship to it is toxic. It may help to know that quitting Facebook doesn't mean the good moments are denied or forgotten. It simply means we need a total break from a relationship that has slowly, and perhaps subtly, eroded our souls.

Breaking up with Facebook isn't easy. As with any relationship, "*It's complicated.*" That our family, friends, fellow employees, church members, banks, local politicians, and favorite coffee shops are on Facebook adds to the social pressure to remain on the site. When we consider quitting Facebook, we're faced with the prospect of obscurity. We may be left out of party invites. Acquaintances may forget about us. Our friends will have conversations without us. Our outreaches could lose members. We might feel an all-encompassing threat of disconnection. Heck, if we are going to divorce Facebook, perhaps we should just move to the Sahara Desert—*alone*.

Widespread use of Facebook can make severing ties with it feel nearly impossible. Its popularity creates pressure to remain on the site in order to be visible, influential, liked, connected, relevant, and helpful. Pressure to remain on Facebook is perhaps a chief emotional obstacle to quitting the site. You may feel profoundly connected to your Facebook home. In addition, Facebook-related social pressures and expectations are so thick that they can be cut with a knife. Those of us who quit the site might find ourselves misunderstood. We might come across as thinking we are too good for Facebook. We may appear to not care about our Facebook connections. We might look like quitters who just couldn't handle the site. Then there's the fear our Facebook friends will miss us or feel frustrated or inconvenienced by having to use email to contact us. We wonder if they'll be sad about not seeing our photos and news anymore. We're scared our group members and page *like*rs will feel abandoned or miss our posts when we leave the site.

I have very good news for you. All of these fears evaporate *once you delete Facebook.*

The fear that people on Facebook will miss you fades once you are gone from the site. The worry that people will be pining for your photos and updates disappears. The sense of obligation to your group members and page *like*rs vanishes like lightning.

Regardless of how real your Facebook connections feel right now, that feeling disintegrates once you are off the site. You will soon forget that your Facebook profile, page, or group ever held any importance. Your pixelated Facebook reality will dissolve into nothingness. What will appear in its place is the fresh air and vibrant colors of the real earth you are standing on.

You will forget about Facebook.

When you delete your account, you also delete every one of those social pressures and expectations you might feel right now. And the world of Facebook will keep turning without you.

Really.

Have you ever felt obligated to engage your Facebook friends, page *likers*, or group members to keep them interested in you or your content? You may wonder if you will fail them if you leave the site. Would you choose to delete Facebook if you knew for sure that its built-in pressures would disappear along with your account?

11
FILING THE PAPERS

One of the reasons we use Facebook is to stay connected. Therefore, if you have chosen to leave Facebook, you may want to make the transition easier for yourself by sending a Facebook or email message to those you'd like to stay connected to. Let them know you are leaving the site, that they are important to you, and that you'd like to keep in touch. Give them your contact information, and ask them for their most up-to-date information. You could state that you look forward to spending time with them in person, over the phone, and through email.

A note such as this accomplishes a few important things. First, you are letting your Facebook friends know they matter so that they will not take it personally when they no longer see you on Facebook. Your message is a compliment to them. Second, you are taking care of the logistics of exchanging contact information. Lastly, you are creating for yourself a sense of closure before permanently deleting your account. This sense of closure will help calm any fears you have of quitting the site.

When letting your Facebook friends know you are leaving, you are not obligated to share why you are making this decision. After all, there may be many reasons. Or your reasons may feel too personal to share in a group message. Someone may reply to your message and ask you why you are quitting. Though you are not obligated to share a reason at all, a generic reason may suffice. You can say that deleting your Facebook account will help you with your time management. Or that deleting your account will enable you to spend more in-person time with others. The important thing to remember is that you don't have to share anything that may feel stressful for you to share. After all, conversations over Facebook about hot button topics (such as Facebook) is one of the things you may look forward to leaving behind as you walk away. This positive change you are making for yourself is bringing you freedom, and you might not want to ruffle any feathers on your way out the door. Keeping your thoughts about Facebook largely to yourself, if that is what you prefer, could help you feel more peaceful as you end your relationship with Facebook.

***

Are you ready to quit Facebook?

If so, here are a few tips to make it a smooth operation:

- Download to your hard drive any photos or videos you have been tagged in that you want to keep but only have access to via someone's else's Facebook photo album.

- Write a list of the reasons you are quitting Facebook. Use declarative statements like *I want to live in the present moment* or *I want a newsfeed-free life* or *I don't want a reason to take any more selfies*. Read this list anytime you want to reassure yourself of your resolve to quit the site.
- Search online to obtain the most current instructions on permanently deleting your Facebook account.

Once you have contacted your Facebook friends and have in front of you the most up-to-date instructions for permanently deleting your Facebook account, you are ready to take action!

Really.

Are you leaving Facebook and stressed about how to tell your Facebook friends? On a recent road trip, I encountered a wallpaper of quotes in a travel plaza; one of them was the Calvin Coolidge quote, "You don't have to explain something you never said." When telling others you will no longer be on Facebook, you can say as little as you want, omitting any statement you might feel an urge to explain later.

12
OLD FLAMES

Now that the divorce is final, there is space in my life for both new loves and old flames. And by *old flames*, I mean the things I used to enjoy to the full before I ever had a Facebook account.

As I write this, I am sitting on my back porch looking at the the winter tree branches that loom high in my yard. My coffee is still warm and the temperature is in the 50s, unusual for December. The sun is shining bright and my face is soaking it in. I am imagining what this yard will look like years from now, whether I will still be living here to enjoy it, and what might transpire between now and then. I am completely basking in the present moment.

I am also grateful. I am grateful for the time I had with Facebook and everything it gave me during that ten-year relationship. But I am even more grateful for my life as it is now, without Facebook. If I hadn't quit Facebook, I likely wouldn't have had as productive a year as I did with reading, writing projects, and photography opportunities. If I was still on Facebook, I believe I would be sitting here feeling anxious about unwanted information I could access with just a few clicks. I'd be taking a picture of the bird on my fence and uploading it along with a status about the warm December weather. I might be scrolling the newsfeed, getting caught up in a shuffle of pages, articles, updates, and photos, then taking care of Facebook maintenance needs. I'd be thinking about the lives of the people behind the updates and photos I just saw. Rather than relaxing fully in the present moment, Facebook would be in my thoughts and on my to-do list.

I am so happy that isn't my life anymore. My plate has been cleared of that large chunk of real estate that is Facebook, and I feel so relieved that logging in isn't a possibility. I have rediscovered many sources of joy since quitting. I have built genuine offline relationships with amazing people. I have shared more of myself with those I had known for years but hadn't spent intentional time with. I feel *more* connected in my relationships than I did when I was on the site. My life has simplicity and peace and less distractions than ever. I never fear I am missing out. I don't wish to be visible, influential, liked, connected, relevant, or helpful on Facebook. Last and not least, I have significantly less anxiety.

I have taken you on a short journey down my path to divorcing Facebook. I shared my reflections because they are not only about me but also about others. If you, too, would be happier without Facebook, I sincerely hope my little book has empowered, inspired, and guided you toward divorcing the site. If you have decided to quit Facebook, I am excited about the freedom you will know when ending a relationship that has been less than healthy for you. Any time we sever toxic relationships and circumstances, we become more alive and can be our best selves again. We may accomplish much more when we are unhampered by the burden of something that was weighing us down. Surprisingly good things can stem from setting boundaries and making right decisions.

I hope that list of good things for you will stretch for miles.

Really.

In spite of our massive world population, I believe your life has a ripple effect that impacts more people in more ways than you know. How you choose to spend your time, your decision to be present in your moments, and your inner peace changes the world. You really can decide to make the changes that will be life-giving for you and tune out all voices discouraging those changes. REALLY.

Divorcing Facebook? Really!? is self-published. You can find it on Amazon.com. If you believe my book may benefit someone, I wonder if you might be willing to take a moment to rate and review it on Amazon. Your honest review will help make my book more likely to be discovered and read by others. Your opinion makes a difference! Thank you. -Audrey

ABOUT THE AUTHOR

Audrey Wagner is the author of *Klonopin Withdrawal and Howling Dogs: Maybe it was God* and *Sleep While You're Still Alive: Good News from a Former Insomniac*, both available on Amazon.com. Audrey has an undergraduate degree in Philosophy and graduate degrees in Counseling and Theological Studies. She enjoys reading, writing, photography, nature, church, and time with family and friends. You can visit Audrey at her Amazon Author Page.

www.ingramcontent.com/pod-product-compliance
Lightning Source LLC
Chambersburg PA
CBHW031359040426
42444CB00005B/346